GW00493887

Copyright © Fischer Fine Art
This edition first published
by Lund Humphries Publishers Limited
16 Pembridge Road, London W11
in association with Fischer Fine Art

ISBN 0–85331–592–2

British Library Cataloguing in Publication
Data available

Designed by Richard Hollis
Photographs by Krebs und Kedro
and Prudence Cuming Associates
Editorial Assistant: Claudia Haas
Made and printed in Great Britain
by BAS Printers Limited, Over Wallop,
Stockbridge, Hampshire

Cover illustrations:
Otto Wagner: Stool for the Austrian
Post Office Savings Bank, 1906
Marcel Breuer: Club Chair *B3*, 1925
Pierre Paulin: Easy Chair *577*, 1966

An exhibition
at Fischer Fine Art
London
24 April – 31 May 1991

PIONEERS OF
MODERN FURNITURE

With an introduction by Colin Amery

FISCHER FINE ART
30 King Street, St James's, London SW1Y 6RJ
Telephone 071 – 839 3942
Fax 071 – 930 1062

Fischer Fine Art
in association with
Lund Humphries
London 1991

ACKNOWLEDGEMENTS

This catalogue has greatly benefited from
the generous help with documentation,
photographs, and editorial assistance of many
individuals, but especially we would like to
thank F. Pietersen, Centraal Museum, Utrecht;
Peter Sulzer, Jean Prouvé Archive, University
of Stuttgart; Christopher Wilk, Chief Curator
of the Furniture Department, Victoria & Albert
Museum, London; and Ida van Zijl, Curator of
Design, Centraal Museum, Utrecht.

Colin Amery   # MODERN FURNITURE

What is *modern* furniture? To William Morris the advent of modernism meant the arrival of the
machine that was to destroy all 'joy in the making'. To the Bauhaus the combination of the advantages of mass
production and the virtual abolition of ornament provided designers with a chance to make things that rejoiced
in their function. The curious thing about the idea of modern furniture is that the very term implies that it is
in some way unlike any other furniture. Have our anatomies become modern and changed shape — do we
sit in an especially modern way free of crinolines and formality? Are our bodies so completely functional that
they no longer need comfort but simply appropriate support. Modern Movement designers, like Adolf Loos and
Marcel Breuer, adopted the aesthetic principles of the modern style in a way that did succeed in conditioning
the way we sit in modern chairs, the way we use modern space and way we live in modern houses.

Not many of us are brave enough entirely to abandon the nineteenth century, partly because our
houses and furniture are full of associations. The furniture we live with has an almost anthropomorphic quality:
it has a character that we recognise and like. Yet it was the eighteenth century, the period of the work of the
great furniture designers — Chippendale, Sheraton, Jacob and others — not the period of the modern
movement, that witnessed the emergence of the scientific approach to human posture and important
publications, like Nicholas Andry de Boisregard's *L'Orthopédie, ou l'Art de prévenir et de corriger dans les
Enfants les Déformités du Corps* (Paris 1741), appeared in the medical world.

The range of furniture (almost entirely chairs) that has been gathered together here shows just
how quickly the avant garde becomes the classical. These are pioneering classics — most of which are accepted
now as bench marks. The furniture of Adolf Loos is like his architecture. He is the master of delicately
proportioned symmetry, and each piece of his furniture is a response to the particular room for which it was
designed. The red bentwood chair for the Cafe Museum (no.1) takes up the curves of that room, in a way
that enhances your appreciation of the sinuous qualities of the design; the depression in the back of the chair
is just where your hand wants to go to lift the chair — function meets beauty. The Otto Wagner stool designed
for the Austrian Post Office Savings Bank in Vienna in 1906 (no.3) is so clearly a pioneer. It is hard to imagine
that it is not in production today; while it clearly relates to the 'design grid' of the Viennese building it would
function well anywhere.

Gebrüder Thonet's manufactory was a unique combination of an experimental company and
talented designers that changed the nature of European furniture design. In fact, it is fair to say that many of
their chairs represent the true high point of European furniture design. When Mies van der Rohe designed his
'*Freischwinger*' (no.6) with its sleigh-like curving arms that turn into 'legs', he was clearly adding to the
technology of bentwood the structural possibilities of tubular steel. Although the chair might appear to defy
ergonomics, it in fact offers a pleasing and well-planned comfort, and like all Mies's furniture design has a far
more bravura quality about it than much of his architecture.

Bravura is not the first word that you might apply to the work of Marcel Breuer, but he is
undoubtedly the complete hero of modern furniture design. As an architect he pushed the modern technology

of reinforced concrete into the realm of abstract art. His furniture quietly does the same. His splendid chairs are timeless, and among the most comfortable chairs ever made. During Breuer's two years in partnership with F. R. S. Yorke in London, he designed a new apartment in Hampstead for Mrs Dorothea Ventris.[1] This white, grey, black and brown interior was entirely furnished by Breuer who brought all his Bauhaus experience to bear on the design. He stated clearly what he thought about the principles that should govern furniture design. He felt that furniture should demonstrate the principle that 'elements should receive different forms as a natural consequence of their different structural purpose'.[2] This tenet of modern design acts as probably the best definition there is of modern furniture.

Le Corbusier's chaise longue (no.12) of bent chromed tubular steel is always seen as a classic. It is the chair the modern architect would buy if he could afford it, and indeed a version returned to the manufacturing repertoire in the 1960s. But it was Le Corbusier's combination of leather and chrome that prompted a style that did spread into the popular market — without the design clarity of Corbusier. Corbusier's furniture owes a lot to Breuer's early experiments. It was Corbusier who wanted to get away from the idea of having furniture as something with a personal and limited use. He was keen to call it all 'equipment' and designed standard chairs, tables and sectional shelves that could be used in any of his architectural interiors. There is a big difference between the approach of Le Corbusier (who would not have wanted his standard universal furniture to become art objects) and the desire of an architect like Frank Lloyd Wright who wanted his integral furniture[3] always to be part of the whole design of a particular house.

The influence of Scandinavian designers upon furniture and architecture in the twentieth century is still under appreciated. Architects like Sven Markelius and Alvar Aalto achieved the difficult task of relying upon organic forms and using the materials and techniques that were adapted from earlier craft practices, using wood which was inventively bent and laminated. The solid wooden legs of an Aalto chair or stool bend at the knee in laminated curves of great elegance and structural efficiency. Aalto was able to use the cantilever principle that Mies and Breuer employed in tubular metal, by only using wood.

Charles Eames really utilised the great renewal that designers and architects had brought from Vienna, the Bauhaus and the Finnish woods, and made it more widely available in both America and Europe. Charles Eames and the firm of Herman Miller were (and Herman Miller still is), the great propagandists for modern furniture. It is entirely appropriate that an exhibition like this one at Fischer Fine Art should move from pioneers to propagandists. Eames combined both roles more than many of the others by his serious affinity with the manufacturing process. Perhaps it took an American to move serious modern design right into the corporate world, and to see the advantages of commercial mass production.

The 1960s and 1970s, as represented here by designers like Verner Panton and Joe Colombo, took furniture into a new modular and yet organic world. Their work used moulded plastic and soft materials and managed to create a sense of anthropomorphism that is highly real. The furniture has become more than just a support and almost inhabits the rooms for which it is designed. There is something more emotional about late modern design that suggests that perhaps we weren't quite as comfortable as we imagined with the purely functional formula. This exhibition gives us the chance to see the evolution of furniture design in the twentieth century and it helps us to realise that each piece enshrines in miniature a complete world of design thought. It is that which makes the collecting of furniture so worthwhile. How else can you acquire the microcosms of modernism and take them home?

1. See illustration with cat. no.20

2. Marcel Breuer, 'As Things Stand', *Architectural Review*, vol.78, 1935

3. See Frank Lloyd Wright: *Architectural Drawings and Decorative Art*, Fischer Fine Art, London 1985

1   CHAIR FOR THE *'CAFE MUSEUM'*

Designed by
Adolf Loos
Vienna, 1898
for the *Cafe Museum*

Manufactured by
J. & J. Kohn in 1898/99

Bent beech frame,
stained red and polished
Cane seat
Slotted screws

Height 87cm / $34\frac{1}{4}$in
Width 42.5cm / $16\frac{3}{4}$in
Depth 51cm / 20in
Seat height 44.5cm / $17\frac{1}{2}$in

Stamped: J. & J. Kohn
Paper label of the company
J. & J.Kohn

Literature:
*Deutsche Kunst und
Dekoration*, vol.V, 1899–1900,
p.260
Kunst und Kunsthandwerk,
vol.II, 1899, p.196
Dekorative Kunst, vol.IV, 1899,
p.193 (ill.)
Heinrich Kulka, *Adolf Loos: Das
Werk des Architekten*, Vienna,
1931, p.27 (ills.7, 8)
*Gebogenes Holz: Konstruktive
Entwürfe Wien 1840–1910*,
Asenbaum/Hummel, Vienna,
1979, p.19 (ill.), p.21 (ill.)
Burkhard Rukschcio, Roland
Schachel, *Adolf Loos: Leben
und Werk*, Residenz Verlag,
Salzburg / Vienna, 1982, p.54
(ill.44), pp.418–420 (ill.407)

Cafe Museum, postcard, 1900

No.1

2   ARMCHAIR FOR THE TELEGRAPH OFFICE *'DIE ZEIT'*

Designed by
Otto Wagner
Vienna, 1902 for the
telegraph office *'Die Zeit'*

Manufactured by
J. & J. Kohn in 1902

Bent beech frame,
stained dark brown,
polished
Seat woven with 'Eisengarn'
cord,
Fabric backrest
Aluminium feet and
riveted arm fittings
Slotted screws

Height 78cm / 30¾in
Width 56.5cm / 22¼in
Depth 49.5cm / 19½in
Seat height 45.5cm / 17⅞in

Stamped: J. & J. Kohn,
Teschen Austria
Paper label of the company
J. & J. Kohn

Literature:
Das Interieur, vol.IV, 1903, p.77
(ill.)
Paul Asenbaum, Peter Haiko,
Herbert Lachmayer, Reiner Zettl,
*Otto Wagner: Möbel und
Innenräume*, Residenz Verlag,
Salzburg / Vienna, 1984, p.202
(ills.257, 259)

OBERBAURAT PROF. OTTO WAGNER. STUHL AUS
DEM DEPESCHENSAAL DER „ZEIT". GEBOGENES
BUCHENHOLZ, DUNKEL GEBEIZT. MIT ALUMINIUM-
BESCHLÄGEN. AUSGEFÜHRT VON J. KOHN & Co.

Illustration in *Das Interieur*, 1903

OTTO WAGNER 1902

No.2

3 STOOL
FOR THE AUSTRIAN POST OFFICE SAVINGS BANK

Designed by
Otto Wagner
Vienna, 1906 for the
Austrian Post Office Savings
Bank

Manufactured by
Gebrüder Thonet in 1906

Bent beech frame,
stained brown and polished
Plywood seat,
stained brown and polished
Aluminium rivets,
Slotted screws

Height 47cm / 18½in
Width and depth
42cm/16½in

Literature:
*Fünfundzwanzig Jahre
Postsparkasse*, Verlag der K. K.
Postsparkasse, Vienna, 1908
Christopher Wilk, *Thonet: 150
Years of Furniture*, Barron's,
New York, 1980, p.64, (ill.72)
*Moderne Vergangenheit, 1800–
1900*, Künstlerhaus Vienna,
1981, p.264 (ill.205)
Jugendstil, floral, funktional,
Bayrisches Nationalmuseum,
Munich, 1984, p.157 (ill.320)
Paul Asenbaum, Peter Haiko,
Herbert Lachmayer, Reiner Zettl,
*Otto Wagner: Möbel und
Innenräume*, Residenz Verlag,
Salzburg / Vienna, 1984, p.37
(ill.40), p.208 (ill.264), p.210
(ill.267)
*Bent Wood and Metal
Furniture: 1850–1946*,
American Federation of Art,
New York, 1987, p.248 (ill.,
cat.48)

Main banking hall of the Austrian Post Office Savings
Bank in 1908

No.3

4   CHAIR

Designed by
Gerrit Rietveld
Utrecht, 1925

Made by
Gerard A. van de Groenekan
in 1925/26

Used in the dining area of
the Schroeder House

Bent iron tube frame,
painted silver
Seat and backrest in
plywood, painted red
Rivets, slotted screws,
square nuts

Height 83cm / 32$\frac{5}{8}$in
Width 44.5cm / 17$\frac{1}{2}$in
Depth 47cm / 18$\frac{1}{2}$in
Seat height 46.5cm / 18$\frac{3}{8}$in
Diameter of iron tube
2.2cm / $\frac{7}{8}$in

Literature:
'Meubels van architect
G. Rietveld', in *Het Landhuis*,
1932, p.458
Theodore M. Brown, *The Work
of G. Rietveld, Architect*,
A.W. Bruna & Zoon, Utrecht,
1958, p.94 (ill.106)
H. de Jong, ed, *Stoelen*, T.H.,
Delft, 1974, no.03–22 (ill.)
Daniele Baroni, *Ursprung des
modernen Möbels: Das Werk
Rietvelds*, Deutsche Verlags-
Anstalt, Stuttgart, 1979, p.94
(no.33)
*Stühle aus Stahl: Metallmöbel
1925–40*, Verlag Walter König,
Cologne, 1980, p.106 (ill.1)

Chair for the Schroeder House, 1925
From Mrs Schroeder's
photograph album

Interior of
Row-House in Utrecht,
photograph, 1930–31

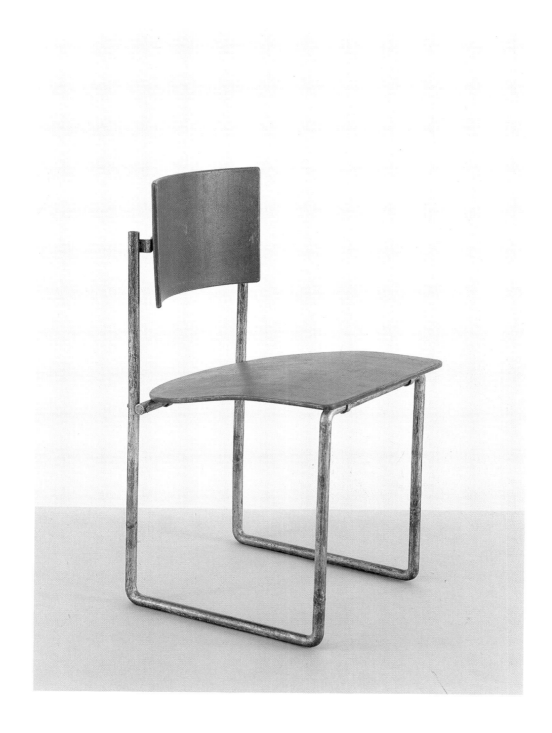

No.4

5 CLUB CHAIR *B 3*

Designed by
Marcel Breuer
Bauhaus, Dessau, 1925

Manufactured by
Gebrüder Thonet, Frankenberg
as model *B 3* from
1929/30 to 1932

Bent steel tube frame,
chromed
Steel stretcher, chromed
Seat, backrests and armrests
in orange 'Eisengarn' fabric
Domed hexagonal screws

Height 75.5cm / 29¾in
Width 77cm/30⅜in
Depth 69cm / 27⅛in
Seat height 44.5cm/17½in
Diameter of steel tube:
2cm / ¾in
Fabric:
Seat
52 × 41.5cm / 20½ × 16⅜in
Backrest
77 × 12cm / 30⅜ × 4¾in
Armrests
68 × 8cm / 26¾ × 3⅛in

Literature:
Thonet catalogue, 1929/30,
model *B3*
Christopher Wilk, *Marcel
Breuer: Furniture and Interiors*,
Museum of Modern Art, New
York, 1981, pp.37–40, (fig. 26)
*Bent Wood and Metal
Furniture: 1850–1946*,
American Federation of Art,
New York, 1987, p.271 (ill.,
cat.67b) and see p.153
(fig.5–54)
Alexander von Vegesack,
*Deutsche Stahlrohrmöbel: 650
Modelle aus Katalogen von
1927–1958*, Bangert Verlag,
Munich, 1986, pp.17, 72 (ill.)
*Sitz-Gelegenheiten: Bugholz-
und Stahlrohrmöbel von
Thonet*, Germanisches
Nationalmuseum, Nuremberg,
1989, pp.96, 104, 244 and see
p.245 (ill.181)

Cover,
Thonet catalogue,
1929/30

Alvar Aalto's apartment in Turku, Finland, photo, 1928

No.5

Designed by
Mies van der Rohe
Bauhaus, Dessau, 1927

Manufactured by
Mücke-Melder,
Czechoslovakia,
under licence from
Gebrüder Thonet
as model *MR 534*
from 1932 to 1936

MR 534
THONET
Entwurf Miës van der Rohe
D.R.P. 467 242

From Thonet catalogue, 1935

Bent steel tube frame,
nickeled
Steel stretcher, nickeled
Wood armrests stained black
and polished
Seat and backrest in red
'Eisengarn' fabric
Domed slotted screws,
domed hexagonal nuts and
bolts

Height 78cm / 30¾in
Width 55.2cm / 21¾in
Depth 85cm / 33⅜in
Seat height 45cm / 17⅛in
Diameter of steel tube:
2.5cm / 1in
Fabric:
Seat
51.5 × 42cm / 20¼ × 16½in
Backrest
50 × 20cm / 19⅝ × 7⅞in

Metal label of the company
Mücke-Melder, Frystat,
CRS

Literature:
Thonet catalogue, 1932 and
1935, see model *MR 534*
Werner Gräff, *Innenräume*, in
association with the Deutscher
Werkbund, Stuttgart, 1928, see
p.26 (ill.53)
Christopher Wilk, *Thonet: 150
Years of Furniture*, Barron's,
New York, 1980, see p.106
(ill.138)
Alexander von Vegesack,
*Deutsche Stahlrohrmöbel: 650
Modelle aus Katalogen 1927–
1958*, Bangert Verlag, Munich,
1986, see pp.103, 106 (ill.)

From Thonet catalogue, 1932

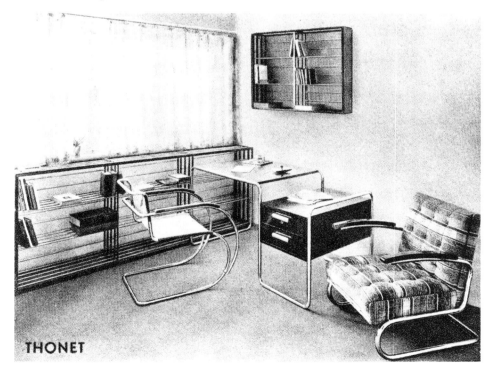

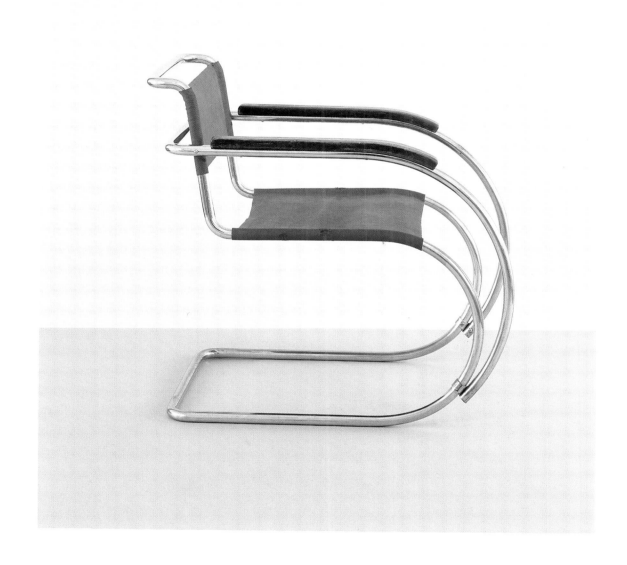

No.6

Designed by
Mies van der Rohe
Bauhaus, Dessau, 1927

Manufactured by
Gebrüder Thonet
as model *MR 533*
from 1932 to 1936

Bent steel tube frame,
chromed
Steel stretcher, chromed
Seat and backrest in red
'Eisengarn' fabric
Domed slotted screws

Height 79cm / $31\frac{1}{8}$in
Width 46.5cm / $18\frac{3}{8}$in
Depth 71.5cm / $28\frac{1}{8}$in
Seat height 45cm / $17\frac{3}{4}$in
Diameter of steel tube
2.5cm / 1in
Fabric:
Seat
46.5 × 40cm / $18\frac{3}{8} \times 15\frac{3}{4}$in
Backrest
43 × 19cm / $17 \times 7\frac{1}{2}$in

Metal label of
the company
Gebrüder Thonet

Literature:
Thonet catalogue, 1932 and
1935, model *MR 533*
Werner Gräff, *Innenräume*, in
association with the Deutscher
Werkbund, Stuttgart 1928, see
p.26 (ill.53)
Philip C. Johnson, *Mies van der
Rohe*, Museum of Modern Art,
New York, 1978, p.49 and p.56
(ill.)
*Sitz-Gelegenheiten: Bugholz-
und Stahlrohrmöbel von
Thonet*, Germanisches
Nationalmuseum, Nuremberg,
1990, pp.96–98

From Thonet catalogue, 1935

MR 533
THONET
Entwurf Miёs van der Rohe
D. R. P. 467 242

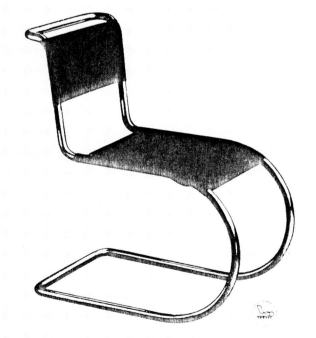

No.7

8   CHAIR *'BEUGELSTOEL'*

Designed by
Gerrit Rietveld
Utrecht, 1927

Manufactured by
Metz & Co., Holland,
from 1930

Bent iron tube frame,
painted blue
Seat in bent plywood,
painted blue
Bolts, hexagonal nuts

Height 73cm / 28¾in
Width 40cm / 15¾in
Depth 56cm / 22in
Seat height 43cm / 17in
Diameter of iron tube
1.6cm / 5.8in

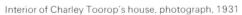

Working drawing, 1927

Literature:
Binnenhuis, vol.10, no.5,
1 March 1928, p.71
A.G. Schneck, *Der Stuhl*,
Stuttgart, 1928
Theodore M. Brown, *The Work
of G. Rietveld, Architect*,
Utrecht, 1958, p.175 (ill.,
cat.59) and see p.85 (ill.98)
Daniele Baroni, *Ursprung des
modernen Möbels: Das Werk
Rietvelds*, Deutsche Verlags-
Anstalt, Stuttgart, 1979, pp.114,
115(ill.)
P. Drijver and J. Niemeijer,
*Rietveld Meubles om zelf te
maken/werkboek, How to
construct Rietveld Furniture/
Workbook*, 1986, p.37 (ill.)

Interior of Charley Toorop's house, photograph, 1931

No.8

9   TABLE *B 18*

Designed by
Marcel Breuer
Bauhaus, Dessau, 1928

Manufactured by
Gebrüder Thonet
as model *B 18*
from 1930/31

Bent steel tube frame,
chromed
Rubber spacing pieces
Glass table top
Domed hexagonal screws

Height 60cm / 23⅝in
Diameter 80cm / 31½in
Diameter of iron tube
2cm / ¾in

Literature:
Thonet catalogue, 1930/31,
model *B 18*
Christopher Wilk, *Marcel
Breuer: Furniture and Interiors*,
Museum of Modern Art, New
York, 1981, see p.79 (fig.74),
p.81
Alexander von Vegesack,
*Deutsche Stahlrohrmöbel: 650
Modelle aus Katalogen von
1927–1958*, Bangert Verlag,
Munich, 1986, see p.20 (ill.),
p.81 (ill.)

From letterhead,
Thonet Company,
1930/31

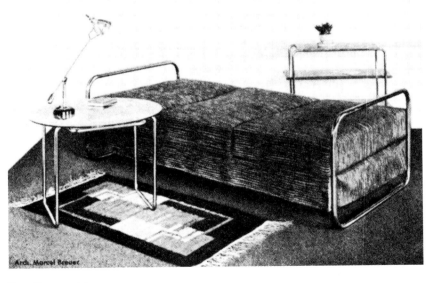

From Thonet catalogue,
1930/31

No.9

Designed by
Bruno Weil (Béwé)
Paris, 1928/29

Manufactured by
Gebrüder Thonet
as model *B 282*
from 1930

Bent steel tube frame,
chromed
Table top and drawers
in beech, painted cream
Aluminium handles
Domed slotted screws

Height 77cm / 30$\frac{3}{8}$in
Width 136cm / 53$\frac{1}{2}$in
Depth 76cm / 30in
Diameter of iron tube
2cm / $\frac{3}{4}$in

Stamped : THONET FABRIQUE
EN TCHECOSLOVAQUIE

Literature :
Thonet catalogue, 1930/31,
model *B 282*, also illustrated
on cover
Christopher Wilk, *Thonet: 150
Years of Furniture*, Barron's,
New York, 1980, p.98 (ill.127),
p.109 (ill.141)
Alexander von Vegesack,
*Deutsche Stahlrohrmobel: 650
Modelle aus Katalogen von
1927 bis 1958*, Bangert Verlag,
Munich, 1986, p.85 (ill.)
*Bent Wood and Metal Furniture
1850–1946*, American
Federation of Art, New York,
1987, p.290 (fig.81c)

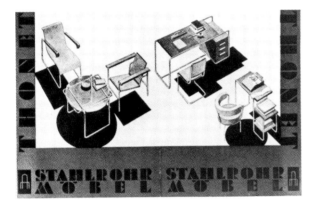

Cover, Thonet catalogue,
1930/31

From Thonet leaflet,
1930/31

BRUNO WEIL (BÉWÉ) 1928/29

No.10

11   **OFFICE CABINET *B 290***

Designed by
Bruno Weil (Béwé)
Paris, 1928/29

Manufactured by
Gebrüder Thonet
as model *B 290*
from 1930

Bent steel tube frame,
chromed
Drawers, shelves and
compartment in beech
and plywood,
painted cream
Sliding glass doors
Aluminium handles
Domed slotted screws

Height 131cm / 51½in
Width 149cm / 58⅝in
Depth 60cm / 23⅝in
Diameter of iron tube
2cm / ¾in

Literature:
Thonet catalogue, 1930/31,
see model *B 290*
Christopher Wilk, *Thonet: 150
Years of Furniture*, Barron's,
New York, 1980, see p.109
(ill.141)
Alexander von Vegesack,
*Deutsche Stahlrohrmöbel: 650
Modelle aus Katalogen von
1927–1958*, Bangert Verlag,
Munich, 1986, see p.92 (ill.)
*Bent Wood and Metal Furniture
1850–1946*, American
Federation of Art, New York,
1987, see p.290 (fig.81c)
*Sitz-Gelegenheiten: Bugholz-
und Stahlrohrmöbel von
Thonet*, Germanisches
Nationalmuseum, Nuremberg,
1990, p.46 (ill.64)

Exhibition room,
Thonet, Paris,
photograph 1930

No.11

Designed by
Le Corbusier, Pierre
Jeanneret and
Charlotte Perriand
Paris, 1928

Manufactured by
Embru-Werke AG,
Rüti, Zurich, as model *2072*
from 1932

Bent steel tube frame,
chromed
Iron base painted green,
rubber feet
Bed in white fabric
with headrest and footrest in
black leather
Slotted screws, iron loops
and springs

Height 66cm / 26in
Width 54cm / 21¼in
Length 159cm / 62⅝in
Diameter of steel tube
2.5cm / 1in

Literature:
Art et Décoration, December
1929, Salon d'Automne issue
Embru-Werke catalogue, Rüti,
Zurich, 1936, model *2072*
*Stühle aus Stahl: Metallmöbel
1925–1940*, Verlag Walter
König, Cologne, 1980, see p.74
(ill.5), p.75
Frank Russell, Philippe Garner,
John Read, *A Century of Chair
Design*, Rizzoli, New York,
1985, see pp.136, 137
Alexander von Vegesack,
*Deutsche Stahlrohrmöbel: 650
Modelle aus Katalogen von
1927–1958*, Bangert Verlag,
Munich, 1986, see p.82 (ill.)
*Bent Wood and Metal
Furniture: 1850–1946*,
American Federation of Art,
New York, 1987, p.284
(fig.76d)
Friederike Mehlau-Wiebking,
Arthur Rüegg, Ruggero
Tropeano, *Schweizer
Typenmöbel 1925–1935*,
*Sigfried Giedion und die
Wohnbedarf AG*, gta Verlag,
Zurich, 1989, p.22 (ill.24), p.45
(ill.8, 9), p.147 (ill.)

From Embru catalogue, 1936

Interior in 'Clarté' apartment house, photograph 1932

No.12

13   WRITING DESK

Designed by
Sven Markelius
Stockholm, 1930

Manufactured by
Nordiska Kompaniet
in 1930

Beech, lacquered orange
Black linoleum writing
surface
Filing pocket with white
metal stretchers and wire
Slotted screws

Height 74cm / $29\frac{1}{8}$in
Width 114cm / $44\frac{7}{8}$in
Depth 55cm / $21\frac{5}{8}$in

Metal label:
A.8.NORDISKAKOMPANIET
R.D 1–C22246

Literature:
Eva Rudberg, *Sven Markelius,
arkitekt*, Arkitektur Förlag,
Stockholm, 1989, p.63 (ill.)

Interior exhibited at Stockholm Fair, 1930

Interior exhibited at Stockholm Fair, 1930

No.13

14 ARMCHAIR *41 'PAIMIO'*

Designed by
Alvar Aalto
Turku, Finland, 1931/32

Manufactured by
Huonekalu-ja
Rakkennustyötehdas Oy,
Turku, Finland,
as model *41*
from 1932

Bent laminated birch and
solid birch frame,
lacquered
Seat in bent plywood,
stained black and lacquered
Slotted screws

Height 67cm/26$\frac{3}{8}$in
Width 60cm / 23$\frac{5}{8}$in
Depth 84cm / 33in
Seat height 31cm / 12$\frac{1}{4}$in

Literature:
Alvar Aalto Furniture, Museum
of Finnish Architecture, Finnish
Society of Crafts and Design,
Artek, Helsinki, 1984, p.76
(ill.103), p.86 (ill.139), p.87
(ills.142, 144), p.88 (ill.145)
Frank Russell, Philippe Garner,
John Read, *A Century of Chair
Design*, Rizzoli, New York,
1985, p.140 (ill.)
*Bent Wood and Metal
Furniture: 1850–1946*,
American Federation of Art,
New York, 1987, p.151 (fig.5–
51), p.312 (fig.101A)

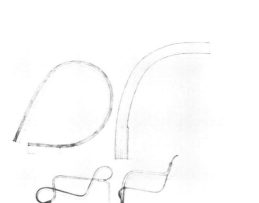

Working drawing, 1930

Aalto furniture exhibited
at the Building Congress for the Nordic Countries,
Helsinki, 1932

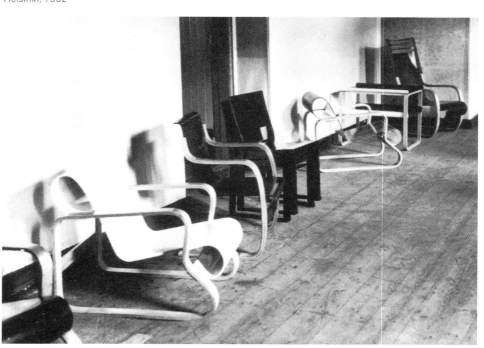

No.14

15   ARMCHAIR *31*

Designed by
Alvar Aalto
Turku, Finland, 1931/32

Manufactured by
Huonekalu-ja
Rakennustyötehdas Oy,
Turku, Finland,
as model *31* from 1932

Distributed by Finmar

Bent, laminated birch and
solid birch frame, lacquered
Seat in bent plywood,
stained black and lacquered

Height 67cm / 26⅜in
Width 60cm / 23⅝in
Depth 77cm / 30⅜in
Seat height 38cm / 15in

Label:
Finmar LTD
Design R.787811–19
PATENT APPLIED FOR
MADE IN FINLAND

Literature:
Alvar Aalto Furniture, Museum
of Finnish Architecture, Finnish
Society of Crafts and Design,
Artek, Helsinki, 1984, p.77
(ill.104), p.87 (ill.144), p.88
(ill.145)
*Bent Wood and Metal
Furniture: 1850–1946*,
American Federation of Art,
New York, 1987, p.151 (fig.5–
52), p.160 (fig.5–68), p.311
(ill., cat.100)
Friederike Mehlau-Wiebking,
Arthur Rüegg, Ruggero
Tropeano, *Schweizer
Typenmöbel 1925–1935:
Sigfried Giedion und die
Wohnbedarf AG*, gta Verlag,
Zurich, 1989, p.92 (ill.49)

Aalto furniture exhibited
at the Museum of Modern Art,
New York, 1938

Aalto furniture exhibited
at the Museum of Modern Art,
New York, 1938

16 SHELF-TABLE *111*

Designed by
Alvar Aalto
Turku, Finland, 1935/36

Manufactured by
Huonekalu-ja
Rakkenustyötehdas Oy,
Turku, Finland,
as model *111* from 1936

Distributed by Finmar

Bent laminated birch,
lacquered
Plywood, stained in part
black,
lacquered

Height 54.6cm / $21\frac{1}{2}$in
Width 83cm / $32\frac{3}{4}$in
Depth 30cm / $11\frac{3}{4}$in

Literature:
*Decorative Art 1937: Year Book
of 'The Studio'*, London, 1937
Alvar Aalto Furniture, Museum
of Finnish Architecture, Finnish
Society of Crafts and Design,
Artek, Helsinki, 1984, p.127
(ill.)

Finmar advertisement
in *Decorative Art 1937*

Dining Table in curled
birch.
£9 0s. 0d.
Dining Chair padded
and covered (exclusive
material).
£3 10s. 0d.
Sideboard, 5 ft.
£14 10s. 0d.
Serving Table.
£1 5s. 0d.
Occasional Table
(Black Top)
17s. 0d.

Frame Chair up-
holstered.
£5 5s. 0d.
High Back Spring
Chair (upholstered)
£5 0s. 0d.
both exclusive material.
Side shelves.
£5 17s. 6d.
Round Table (Black
top): £1 15s. 0d.
Stool. 8s. 6d.
Book Case.
£4 15s. 0d.

A Finmar chair interprets the beauty and
comfort of curves .... A Finmar table is a
very practical essay in modern simplicity ....

No.16

17   ARMCHAIR

Designed by
Gerald Summers
before 1934

Manufactured by
Makers of Simple Furniture
Ltd, London,
from 1934

Bent plywood, lacquered

Height 76.5cm / 30⅛in
Width 61cm / 24in
Depth 86.5cm / 34in
Seat height: 31cm / 12¼in

Literature:
Art and Decoration, November
1934, p.59 (ill.)
Design for Today, June 1934,
p.222 (ill.)
Architectural Review, December
1935, p.194 (ill.)
Frank Russell, Philippe Garner,
John Read, *A Century of Chair
Design*, Rizzoli, New York,
1985, p.114 (ill.)
*Bent Wood and Metal
Furniture: 1850–1946*,
American Federation of Art,
New York, 1987, p.318 (ill.,
cat.106)

246, 35 -. Table,
Thonet Bros.,
Left to right:
70, 23 6; A 477,
helf, T 236, 24 -.
wood and cane
A 811 1F, 37 6.

Table veneered with walnut, T 253, £2 17 6.
Obtainable from Thonet Bros., Ltd. **194.**
Armchair cut out of single sheet of plywood,
£3 15 0. Makers of Simple Furniture. **195.**
Birch nesting chair. CIP. Designed by Alvar
Aalto. Lacquered in red, blue or black. 19 -.
Finmar, Ltd.

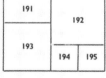

From *Architectural Review*, 1935

No.17

18 *'ZIG ZAG'* CHAIR

Designed by
Gerrit Rietveld
Utrecht, 1934

Made by
Gerard A. van de Groenekan
in 1938
for his personal use

Elm, painted white
Brass slotted screws,
hexagonal nuts

Height 72cm / 28¾in
Width 38cm / 15in
Depth 42cm / 16½in
Seat height 41cm / 16⅛in

Stamped:
H.G.M.
G.A.v.d.GROENEKAN
DE BILT NEDERLAND

Literature:
De 8 en Opbouw, vol.6, no.1,
January 1935, pp.1–8
Bouwkundig Weekblad, vol.56,
no.47, 23 November 1935,
p.488
Theodore M. Brown, *The Work
of G. Rietveld, Architect*,
A. W. Bruna & Zoon, Utrecht,
1958, p.102 (ill.), pp.103, 104
(ill.122), p.115 (ill.144), p.116
(ill.146), p.177 (ill., cat.73)
Daniele Baroni, *Ursprung des
modernen Möbels: Das Werk
Rietvelds*, Deutsche Verlags-
Anstalt, Stuttgart, 1979, p.130
(ill.), p.133 (ill.), p.134 (ill.),
p.135 (ill.)

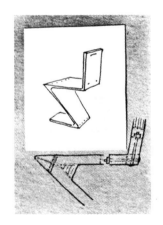

Working drawing, 1934

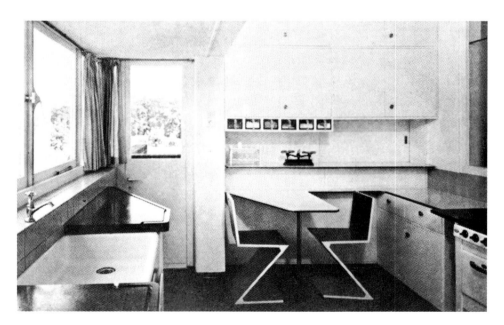

Interior, in Stoop Family House, Velp,
photograph 1950

No.18

19   LOUNGE CHAIR *313*

Designed by
Marcel Breuer
Zurich, 1932

Manufactured by
Embru-Werke AG,
Rüti, Zurich, as model *313*
from 1934

Distributed by Wohnbedarf,
Zurich

Bent aluminium frame
and aluminium slats
Beech armrests
painted black
Slotted bolts,
square nuts,
rivets

Height 75cm/29½in
Width 60cm / 23⅝in
Length 145cm / 57in

Literature:
*Das federnde Aluminium-
Möbel*, Wohnbedarf, Zurich,
1933, illustrated on cover and
no.313
*Stühle aus Stahl: Metallmöbel
1925–1940*, Verlag Walter
König, Cologne, 1980, p.67
(ill.14)
Christopher Wilk, *Marcel
Breuer: Furniture and Interiors*,
Museum of Modern Art, New
York, 1981, see p.125 (figs.124
and 125)
Alexander von Vegesack,
*Deutsche Stahlrohrmöbel: 650
Modelle aus Katalogen von
1927–1958*, Bangert Verlag,
Munich, 1986, p.122 (ill.),
p.126
Friederike Mehlau-Wiebking,
Arthur Rüegg, Ruggero
Tropeano, *Schweizer
Typenmöbel 1925–1935:
Sigfried Giedion und die
Wohnbedarf AG*, gta Verlag,
Zurich, 1989, p.49 (ills.3, 4),
p.65 (ill.4), p.93 (ill.50),
p.142(ill.)

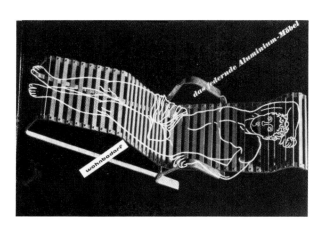

Cover, Wohnbedarf catalogue,
Das federnde Aluminium-Möbel,
1933

Advertising photograph for
Breuer's aluminium programme by Wohnbedarf,
1934

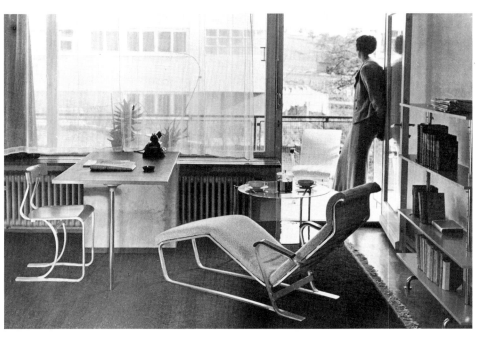

No.19

20   CHAISE LONGUE

Designed by
Marcel Breuer
England, 1935

Manufactured by
Isokon Furniture Co, London,
from 1936

Bent laminated birch frame,
lacquered
Bent plywood seat,
lacquered
Height 76cm / 30in
Width 61cm / 24in
Length 143cm / 56¼in

Label:
ISOKON FURNITURE Co.
Tele. PRI. 5562 London N.W.3.
ISOKON. LONG CHAIR
PAT. NO. 478138
REGD. NO. 812856
Made in England

Literature:
Christopher Wilk, *Marcel
Breuer: Furniture and Interiors*,
Museum of Modern Art,
New York, 1981, p.126, p.127
(fig.126), p.145 (fig.147)
*Bent Wood and Metal
Furniture: 1850–1946*,
American Federation of Art,
New York, 1987, p.159 (fig.5–
67), p.321 (ill.109), p.322
(fig.109A)

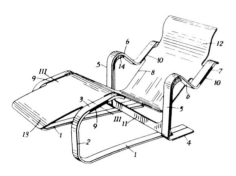

Working drawing, 1936

Ventris apartment, London, 1936

No.20

21   NESTING TABLES

Designed by
Marcel Breuer
England, 1936

Manufactured by
Isokon Furniture Company,
London,
from 1936

Bent plywood,
painted cream

Three pieces

Largest table:
Height 38cm / 15in
Width 46cm / 18in
Length 61cm / 24in

Literature:
Christopher Wilk, *Marcel Breuer: Furniture and Interiors*, Museum of Modern Art, New York, 1981, p.134 (fig.131), p.149 (fig.153)
Fiona McCarthy, *British Design since 1889*, London, 1982, see p.106 (ill.)

Marcel Breuer's house in Lincoln, Massachusetts,
photograph 1939

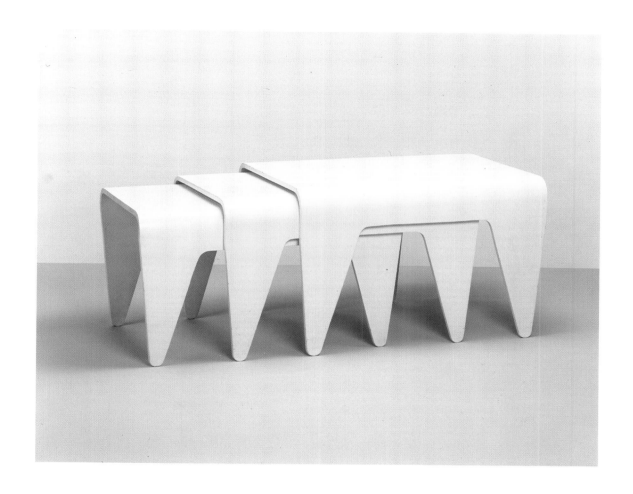

No.21

Designed by
Jean Prouvé
Nancy, France, 1942

Manufactured by
Les Ateliers Jean Prouvé S.A.,
Nancy, from 1942

Bent iron tube legs
and arms, painted green
Armrests and feet in oak,
lacquered
Seat and backrest in
sheet-zinc and oak,
lacquered
Domed brass slotted screws
Iron bar with
hexagonal screws

Height 93.5cm / 36$\frac{7}{8}$in
Width 68cm / 26$\frac{3}{4}$in
Depth 95cm / 37$\frac{3}{8}$in
Seat height 33cm / 13in

Literature:
Domus, no.283, 1953, p.25 (ill.)
Yolande Amic, *Intérieurs: Le mobilier français 1945–1964*, Paris, 1983, see p.69 (ill.)
H. de Jong, ed., *Stoelen*, T.H., Delft, 1974, no.04–XX (ill.)
Jean Prouvé, Serge Mouille: Two Master Metal Workers, New York / Paris, 1985, see p.51 (ill.), p.56 (ill.), see p.57 (ill.)
Jean Prouvé: Meubles 1924–1953, Musée des Arts Décoratifs de Bordeaux, 1989, p.26 (ill.), p.27 (ill.), p.40 (ill.)
Jean Prouvé 'Constructeur', Centre Georges Pompidou, Paris, 1990, p.116 (ill.)

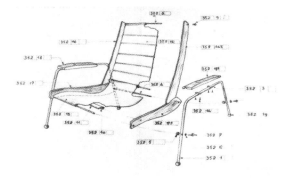

Working drawing, 1942

Interior at *Exposition des Arts Ménagers*, 1951

No.22

23   CHAIR *300*

Designed by
Jean Prouvé
Nancy, France, c.1948

Manufactured by
Ateliers Jean Prouvé S.A.,
Nancy, as model *300*
from 1948

Distributed by
Steph Simon, Paris

Bent tubular iron
and iron frame,
painted red-brown
Black rubber feet
Seat and backrest in
plywood, lacquered
Domed slotted screws,
plugs, hexagonal nuts
Iron bar with hexagonal
screws

Height 80cm / 31½in
Width 41.5cm / 16⅜in
Depth 47cm / 18½in
Seat height 47.5cm / 18¾in

Construction drawing, 8.1.1952

Literature:
Domus, no.283, 1953, p.25 (ill.)
Domus, no.293, 1954, p.22
(ill.), p.23 (ill.)
Stoelen, T.H., Delft, 1974,
no.04–14 (ill.)
Yolande Amic, *Intérieurs:
Le mobilier français 1945–64*,
Paris, 1983, p.69 (ill.)
*Jean Prouvé, Serge Mouille,
Two Master Metal Workers*,
New York / Paris, 1985, see
p.44 (ill.), p.45 (ill.), p.51 (ill.)
*Jean Prouvé: Meubles 1924–
1953*, Musée des Arts Décoratifs
de Bordeaux, 1989, p.21 (ill.),
p.22 (ill.)
Jean Prouvé 'Constructeur',
Centre Georges Pompidou,
Paris, 1990, p.128 (ills.33, 34)

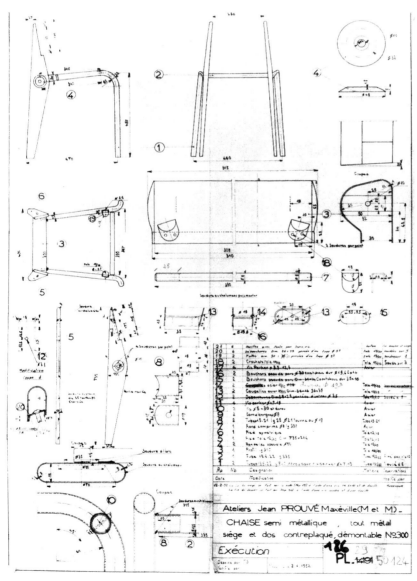

No.23

Designed by
Jean Prouvé
Nancy, France, 1950,
for the University of
Strasbourg

Manufactured by
Les Ateliers Jean Prouvé S.A.,
Maxéville, 1950 to 1954

Distributed by Steph Simon,
Paris

Bent tubular iron and
iron frame, painted black
Seat in bent plywood,
lacquered
Aluminium screws

Height 87cm / $34\frac{1}{4}$in
Width 50cm / $19\frac{5}{8}$in
Depth 70cm / $27\frac{1}{2}$in
Seat height 42cm / $16\frac{1}{2}$in

Literature:
Jean Prouvé, Serge Mouille:
Two Master Metal Workers,
New York / Paris, 1985, p.54
(ill.) p.55 (ill.)
Jean Prouvé: Meubles 1924–
53, Musée des Arts Décoratifs
de Bordeaux, 1989, p.32 (ill.)

Advertising leaflet, Steph Simon, Paris, 1950s

No.24

25 TABLE *'CAFÉTERIA'*

Designed by
Jean Prouvé
Nancy, France, 1950
for the Cité Universitaire des
Arts et Métiers

Manufactured by
Les Ateliers Jean Prouvé S.A.,
Maxéville,
from 1951 to 1954

Distributed by Steph Simon,
Paris

Iron legs,
painted red-brown
Rubber feet
Table top in softwood,
green linoleum,
anodised aluminium trim
Slotted screws,
hexagonal screws

Height 74cm / 29⅛in
Diameter 95cm / 37⅜in

Literature:
L'Architecture d'Aujourd'hui,
37, October 1951, p.XLVI (ill.)
*Jean Prouvé: Meubles 1924–
1953*, Musée des Arts Décoratifs
de Bordeaux, 1989, p.30 (ill.)

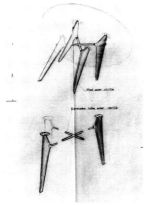

Working drawing, 29 June 1950

Advertisement by Steph Simon, Paris, 1951

No.25

Designed by
Jean Prouvé
and Charlotte Perriand
Nancy, France, 1952,
for the Maison du Méxique,
Paris

Polychrome design of
lacquered surface by
Sonia Delaunay

Manufactured by
Les Ateliers Jean Prouvé S.A.,
Nancy,
in 1953/54

Pine shelves and feet,
lacquered
Doors in fibreboard,
lacquered yellow and blue
Compartments in
aluminium,
lacquered black and white
Iron rods and nuts

Height 165cm / 65in
Width 185cm / 72$\frac{7}{8}$in
Depth 30cm / 11$\frac{3}{4}$in

Literature:
Domus, no.293, 1954, see p.23
(ill.)
Yolande Amic, *Intérieurs:
Le mobilier français 1945–64*,
Paris, 1983, p.68 (ill.)
*Jean Prouvé: Meubles 1924–
1953*, Musée des Arts Décoratifs
de Bordeaux, 1989, p.20 (ill.)
Jean Prouvé 'Constructeur',
Centre Georges Pompidou,
Paris, 1990, p.187 (ill.)

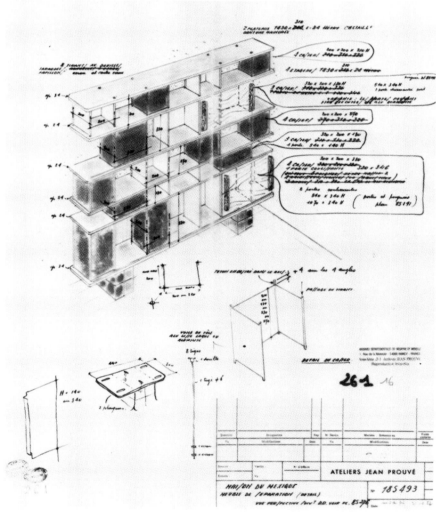

Construction drawing, 21 October 1952

No.26

Designed by
Charles Eames
California, USA, 1946

Manufactured by
Evans Products Company,
Venice, California, USA,
as model *FSW 6* from 1947

Distributed by
Herman Miller Furniture Company,
Zeeland, Michigan

Moulded laminated
plywood, lacquered
Full-length canvas hinges

Height 172cm / 67¾in
Width 162cm / 63¾in
Six panels, each
25cm / 9⅞in

Literature:
*The Collection of Molded
Plywood Furniture designed by
Charles Eames*, catalogue of
Evans Product Co., c.1947,
model *FSW 6*
Collection, catalogue of Herman
Miller Furniture Co., Zeeland,
Michigan, 1952, p.108 (ill.)
Arthur Drexler: *Charles Eames
Furniture from the Design
Collection*, Museum of Modern
Art, New York, 1973, p.20
(ill.32), p.28, p.29 (ills.46, 47,
48)
*Bent Wood and Metal Furniture,
1850–1946*, American
Federation of Art, New York,
1987, pp.330–331 (ill., cat.118)
John Neuhart, Marilyn Neuhart,
Ray Eames, *Eames Design*,
Abrams, New York, 1989, p.76
(ill.), p.77 (ill.)

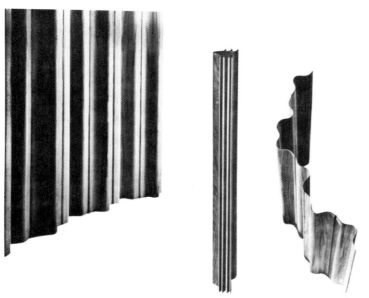

From *Charles Eames Furniture* exhibition catalogue,
Museum of Modern Art, New York, 1973

Installation of Eames furniture by Mies van der Rohe,
Museum of Modern Art, New York, 1947

No.27

Designed by
Charles Eames
California, USA, 1951

Manufactured by
Herman Miller Furniture Co.,
as model *ETR*
from 1952

Distributed by
Herman Miller Furniture Company,
Zeeland, Michigan

Iron supports, chromed
Table top in plywood, with
black plastic laminate
surface
Slotted screws

Height 25cm / 9$\frac{7}{8}$in
Width 174.6cm / 68$\frac{3}{4}$in
Depth 57.2cm / 22$\frac{1}{2}$in

Literature:
Collection, catalogue of Herman
Miller Furniture Co., Zeeland,
Michigan, 1952, p.114 (ill.),
p.115 (ill.)
Roberto Aloi, *Mobili Tipo*,
Ulrico Hoepli, Milan, 1956,
p.103 (ill.)
Cara Greenberg: *Mid-Century
Modern: Furniture of the 1950s*,
Thames & Hudson, London,
1985, pp.86, 87 (ill.)
John Neuhart, Marilyn Neuhart,
Ray Eames, *Eames Design*,
Abrams, New York, 1989, p.149
(ill.)

From Herman Miller catalogue, 1952

Interior with Herman Miller furniture designed by
Charles Eames and George Nelson, 1956

No.28

29 ROCKER *RAR*

Designed by
Charles Eames
California, USA
1950

Manufactured by
Zenith Plastics, California,
for Herman Miller
Furniture Co.
as model *RAR*
from 1950/51

Iron support, chromed,
birch runners
Moulded polyester seat
Rubber shockmounts,
Philips screws,
hexagonal nuts

Height 68cm / 26¾in
Width 63cm / 24⅞in
Depth 66cm / 26in
Seat height 40cm / 15¾in

Label:
DESIGNED BY CHARLES
EAMES, herman miller,
ZEELAND MICHIGAN
SHIPPED FROM VENICE
CALIFORNIA

Distributed by
Herman Miller Furniture Compar
Zeeland, Michigan

Literature:
Collection, catalogue of Herman
Miller Furniture Co., Zeeland,
Michigan, 1952, p.94 (ill.),
p.95 (ill.)
Arthur Drexler, *Charles Eames
Furniture from the Design
Collection*, Museum of Modern
Art, New York, 1973, p.34
(ills.58, 59)
John Neuhart, Marilyn Neuhart,
Ray Eames, *Eames Design*,
Abrams, New York, 1989, p.141
(ill.)

From Herman Miller catalogue, 1952

No.29

Designed by
Verner Panton
Denmark, 1960

Manufactured by
Herman Miller
Furniture Co.,
Zeeland, Michigan, USA
from 1967 to 1975

Moulded polyester and
fibreglass, sprayed white

Six pieces

Height 81cm / 31$\frac{7}{8}$in
Width 50cm / 19$\frac{5}{8}$in
Depth 58.5cm / 23in
Seat height 40cm / 15$\frac{3}{4}$in

Literature:
Gerd Hatje and Elke Kaspar,
eds., *new furniture/neue möbel
9*, Verlag Gerd Hatje, Stuttgart,
1969, ills.18, 19
Karl Mang, *Geschichte des
modernen Möbels*, Verlag Gerd
Hatje, Stuttgart, 1978, p.159
(ill.363)
Design since 1945,
Philadelphia Museum of Art,
Philadelphia, 1983, p.64
(pl.36), p.132
*Möbeldesign: Made in
Germany*, Baden-Württemberg,
Milan, 1986, cat.60.8 (ill.)
Klaus-Jürgen Sembach,
Gabriele Leuthäuser, Peter
Gössel, *Möbeldesign des
20.Jahrhunderts*, Taschen
Verlag, Cologne, undated, p.196
(ill.)

From *new furniture / neue möbel*,
1969

From *Geschichte des modernen Möbels*, 1978

No.30

31   ARMCHAIR *4801/5*

Designed by
Joe Colombo
Milan, 1965

Manufactured by
Kartell USA,
Easley, South Carolina,
as model *4801/5*
from 1965 to 1971

Bent plywood,
painted black
White rubber stoppers

Height 58.5cm / 23in
Width 71cm / 28in
Depth 66cm / 26in
Seat height 33cm / 13in

Literature:
Gerd Hatje and Elke Kaspar,
eds., *new furniture / neue möbel 9*,
Verlag Gerd Hatje, Stuttgart,
1969, p.36 (ills.95, 96)
*Italy: The New Domestic
Landscape*, Museum of Modern
Art, New York, 1972, p.30 (ill.)
Design since 1945, Philadelphia
Museum of Modern Art,
Philadelphia, 1983, p.123 (ill.)

From *Italy: The New Domestic Landscape*,
Museum of Modern Art, New York, 1972

No.31

32   CHAIR AND STOOL *'DJINN'*

Designed by
Olivier Mourgue
Paris, 1965

Manufactured by
Airborne International,
France
from 1965 to 1976

Used in
the space station interior
of Stanley Kubrick's film
2001 : A Space Odyssey in
1968

Steel frame
Upholstered in
polyurethane foam
Covered in green nylon
stretch fabric

Chair:
Height 67cm / 26$\frac{3}{8}$in
Width 65cm / 25$\frac{1}{2}$in
Depth 76cm / 30in
Seat height 38cm / 15in
Stool:
Height 38cm / 15in
Width 66cm / 26in
Depth 58cm / 22$\frac{7}{8}$in

Literature:
Design since 1945, Philadelphia
Museum of Art, Philadelphia,
1983, p.61 (pl.31), p.130
Ted Sennett, *Great Hollywood
Movies*, Abrams, New York,
1983, p.166 (ill.)

Still from Stanley Kubrick's movie,
2001 : A Space Odyssey

No.32

33   EASY CHAIR *577*

Designed by
Pierre Paulin
France, 1966

Manufactured by
Artifort Co.,
Annalaan, Netherlands
as model *577*
from 1966

Steel frame
Upholstered in
polyurethane foam
Covered in orange stretch
fabric

Height 62cm / 24⅜in
Width 90cm/35½in
Depth 94cm / 37in
Seat height 32cm / 12½in

Literature:
Gerde Hatje and Elke Kaspar,
eds., *new furniture/neue möbel
8*, Verlag Gerd Hatje, Stuttgart,
1966, back pages
Gerd Hatje and Elke Kaspar, eds,
new furniture neue möbel 9,
Verlag Gerd Hatje, Stuttgart,
1969, p.18 (ills.33–35)
Design since 1945, Philadelphia
Museum of Art, Philadelphia,
1983, p.132 (ill.)

Artifort advertisement, 1966

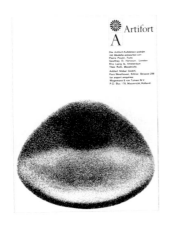

From *new furniture / neue möbel*, 1969

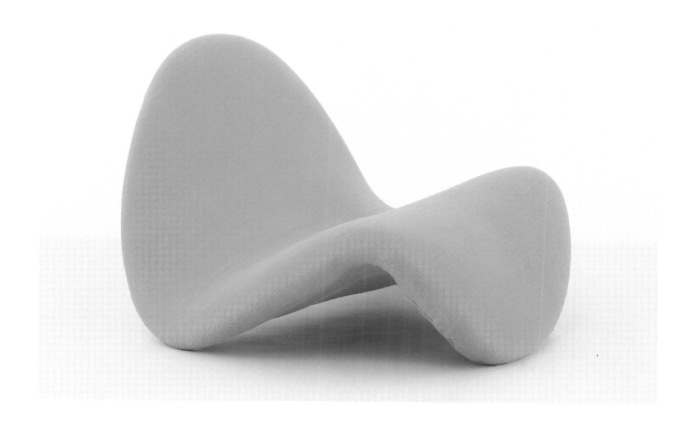

No.33

Designed by
Joe Colombo
Milan, 1968

Manufactured by
Sormani, Italy
from 1968 to 1971

Square section iron tube
frame
Upholstered in
polyurethane foam
Covered in green stretch
fabric
Metal clamps

Large element:
Height 50cm / $19\frac{5}{8}$in
Width 75cm / $29\frac{1}{2}$in
Middle size element:
Height 37cm / $14\frac{1}{2}$in
Width 75cm / $29\frac{1}{2}$in
Small element:
Height 27cm / $10\frac{5}{8}$in
Width 75cm / $29\frac{1}{2}$in

Literature:
Karl Mang, *Geschichte des modernen Möbels*, Verlag Gerd Hatje, Stuttgart, 1978, p.163 (ill.367)
Italy: The New Domestic Landscape, Museum of Modern Art, New York, 1972, p.116 (ill.)
Design since 1945, Philadelphia Museum of Art, Philadelphia, 1983, p.61 (pl.30), p.124 (ill.)

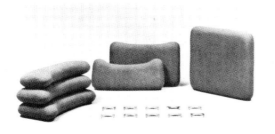 

From *Italy: The New Domestic Landsca[pe]*,
Museum of Modern York, 19[ ]

'Domestic Landscape' illustrated in *Geschichte des modernen Möbels*, 1978

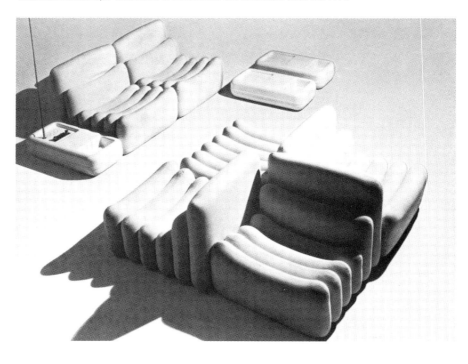

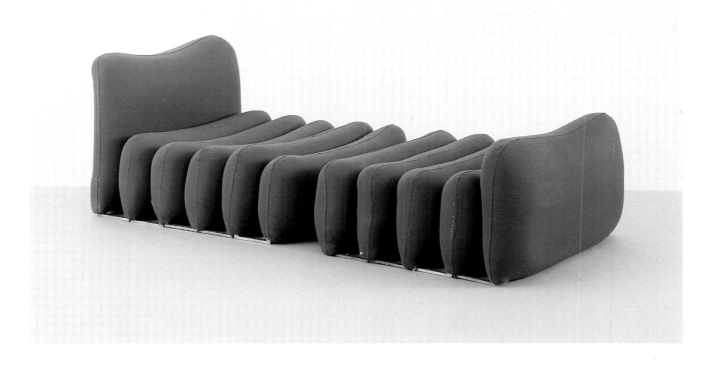

No.34

ADOLF LOOS
Architect, designer and theorist.
Born 1870, Brno. Died 1933, Vienna.
Studied at Technische Hochschule, Dresden.
Extensive trip to the United States of America,
1893–96.
After return opened architectural office in Vienna.
Founded Free School of Architecture, 1906.
Chief housing architect, Vienna, 1920–22.
Loos's buildings include:
Haus am Michaelerplatz, Vienna, 1910.
Steiner House, Vienna, built in concrete, 1910.
Tristan Tzara House, Paris, 1926.
Interiors and furniture include:
Cafe Museum, Vienna, 1898.
Chair (cat.1), the first architectural design in
bentwood.
Kärntner Bar, Vienna, 1907.
Store interiors for Knize, Vienna, 1910–13.
Store interior for Knize, Berlin, 1924.
Store interior for Knize, Paris, 1927–28.
Also several important apartment interiors in
Vienna, Prague, and Paris.

OTTO WAGNER
Architect, teacher.
Born 1841, Vienna. Died 1918, Vienna.
Studied at the Technische Hochschule, Vienna, at
the Bauakademie, Berlin under C.F. Busse and
Akademie der bildenden Künste, Vienna under
August Siccardsburg and Eduard van der Nüll.
Settled as architect in Vienna.
Appointed Professor of special school of
architecture at Akademie der bildenden Künste,
Vienna, 1894.
Wagner's buildings include:
Vienna railway system stations, 1895–98.
Apartment houses, Wienzeile, Vienna, 1898–99.
Church of Steinhof, Vienna, 1905–7.
Post Office Savings Bank, Vienna, 1904–6 and
1910–12.
Lupus Sanatorium, Vienna, 1910–13.
Interiors and furniture designs include:
Telegraph Office *'Die Zeit'*, Armchair (cat.2),
Vienna, 1902. Post Office Savings Bank. Stool
(cat.3), Vienna, 1906.

GERRIT THOMAS RIETVELD
Cabinet maker, designer and architect.
Born 1888, Utrecht. Died 1964, Utrecht.
Apprentice in father's cabinet making shop.
Settled as cabinet maker in Utrecht in 1911.
Member of De Stijl from 1919.
Collaboration with Mrs Truus Schroeder-Schräder
from 1921.
One of the founders of CIAM (Congrès
internationaux d'architecture moderne), La Sarraz,
Switzerland.
From 1930, practising architect in Holland and
abroad.
Rietveld's buildings include:
Schroeder House, Utrecht, 1924.
Row-houses, Utrecht, 1930–31.
Cinema, Vreeburg, 1936.
Stoop Family House, Velp, 1951.
Netherlands Pavilion, Biennale, Venice, 1954.
Vincent van Gogh Museum, Amsterdam, 1963.
Furniture designs include:
Red-blue Chair, 1919.
Chair for the Schroeder House (cat.4), Utrecht,
1925, designed in the same year as the B3
Armchair by Marcel Breuer (cat.5). One of the
earliest pieces of tubular steel furniture, 1927.
Beugelstoel Chair (cat.8).
'Zig-Zag' Chair (cat.18), 1934.

MARCEL BREUER
Architect, furniture and interior designer.
Born 1902, Pécs, Hungary. Died 1981, New York.
After short stay in Vienna, studied at the Bauhaus
in Weimar.
Head of Carpentry Workshop of the Bauhaus in
Dessau, 1925.
Architectural practice in Berlin, 1928–31.
In 1935, moved to England. Partnership with
F.R.S. Yorke in London until 1937. Invitation from
Gropius, then Chairman of Department of
Architecture at Harvard, to join him as Associate
Professor.
Emigrated to USA, 1937. Taught at Harvard
University.
Moved to New York, opened architectural office,
1946.

Breuer's architectural work includes:
One of three architects for the new Unesco
headquarters, Paris, 1953–58.
Abbey of St John, Collegeville, Minnesota,
1953–61.
Centre at La Goude, France, 1960–69.
Whitney Museum of American Art, New York,
1963–66.
IBM Complex at Boca Raton, Florida, 1966–67.
Furniture designs include:
Club Chair B3 ('Wassily') (cat.5) Bauhaus,
Dessau, 1925. First experiments with tubular steel
furniture taking dimensions of tube from bicycle.
With Schroeder House Chair (cat.4), the earliest
tubular steel furniture.
Table B18 (cat.9), Bauhaus, Dessau, 1928.
Lounge Chair 313 (cat.19), Zurich, 1932. One of
the first examples of furniture in aluminium.
Chaise Longue (cat.20), England, 1936. Seat
made of one plywood piece.
Nesting Tables (cat.21), England, 1936.

MIES VAN DER ROHE
Architect, designer.
Born 1886, Aachen, Germany. Died 1969,
Chicago.
No academic training.
After 1905 worked for Bruno Paul, at that time
Germany's leading furniture and interior designer.
In 1908 joined Peter Behrens' architectural office
as apprentice.
Opened own architectural office in Berlin.
First Vice-President of the Deutsche Werkbund,
1926.
In 1927 second exhibition of Weissenhofsiedlung,
Stuttgart, under the direction of Mies van der
Rohe.
Succeeded Hannes Mayer as director of the
Bauhaus in 1930.
Emigrated to the USA, 1937.
In 1938, invitation to teach at Illinois Institute of
Technology, Chicago.
Mies van der Rohe's buildings include:
Weissenhofsiedlung, Stuttgart, 1927.
German Pavilion, International Exhibition,
Barcelona, 1928–29.
Tugendhat House at Brno, Czechoslovakia, 1930.
Campus plans and buildings for Illinois Institute of
Technology, Chicago, 1940.
Lake Shore Drive Apartment, Chicago, 1950–51.
Convention Hall, Chicago, 1953.
Seagram Building, New York, 1954–58.
National Gallery, West Berlin (with Philip
Johnson), 1962–68.
Furniture designs include:
Armchair 534 and Chair 533 *'Freischwinger'* (cat.6
and 7), Bauhaus, Dessau, 1927. With the chair by
Mart Stam, one of the first and most developed
cantilevered chair designs.
'Barcelona' Chair, 1929.

BRUNO WEIL (BÉWÉ)

Austrian designer. Trained as architect.
Director of French branch of the Thonet Company,
Thonet Frères, Paris, 1928–33.
Used the pseudonym 'Béwé' as designer.
Produced designs not only of German but also
progressive French architects, including Le
Corbusier, Charlotte Perriand and André Lurçat.
Weil's stepfather, Leopold Pilzer, became majority
shareholder in Thonet at the end of the Twenties.
Emigrated to USA, 1939.
Béwé's furniture design includes:
Writing Table B282 (cat.10), Paris, 1928/29.
Office Cabinet B290 (cat.11), Paris, 1928/29.
In 1943, under the influence of Charles Eames,
began organic chair program 'Bentply', first
produced in New York, later in France.

LE CORBUSIER

Architect, planner, painter and theorist.
Born 1887, as Charles Édouard Jeanneret, La
Chaux-de-Fonds, Switzerland.
Died 1965, Roquebrune-Cap-Martin, France.
Studied at art school in his home town.
Travelled extensively throughout Europe and the
Middle East.
Short apprenticeship at Peter Behrens's
architectural office in Berlin.
Settled in Paris, 1917.
First exhibition with Amédée Ozenfant; founded
avant-garde magazine with Ozenfant, *L'Esprit
Nouveau*, 1918.
In 1928 Charlotte Perriand began work in
Corbusier's studio.
Studio in southern France, 1940–44.
Le Corbusier's buildings include:
House in the Weissenhofsiedlung, Stuttgart, 1927.
Villa Savoye, Poissy, 1929–31.
Unité d'Habitation, Marseilles, 1947–52.
Collaboration on Unesco Building in Paris, 1953.
Church of Notre Dame du Haut at Ronchamp,
1950–54.
Law Courts and Secretariat, Chandigarh, 1951–56.
Interiors and furniture design include:
Exposition Internationale des Arts Décoratifs in
Paris; *L'Esprit Nouveau* pavilion, furnished with
Thonet bentwood chairs, 1925.
Chaise Longue 2072 (cat.12), Paris, 1928.
Grand Confort Armchair, Paris, 1928.

ALVAR AALTO

Architect, designer.
Born 1898, Kuortane, Finland.
Died 1976, Helsingfors, Finland.
Studied at Polytechnic in Helsinki, as pupil of
Armas Lindgren.
Extensive travelling in Europe.
Opened first architectural office in Jyväskyle in
1923.
Married Aino Marsio, his most important
collaborator, in 1925.
In 1927 moved to Turku, and then to Helsinki.
Active member of CIAM.
Patented a method for bending wood, used in his
three-legged stool, 1933.
Founded Artek Furniture Company, 1935.
1940–46 Taught at Massachusetts Institute of
Technology, College of Architecture, 1940–46.
Aalto's buildings include:
Paimio Sanatorium, 1929–33.
Finnish Pavilion, Paris World's Fair, 1937.
Finnish Pavilion, New York World's Fair, 1939.
Cultural Center, Wolfsburg, 1959–62.
Opera House, Essen, 1963.
Interiors and furniture designs include:
'Paimio' Chair 41 (cat.14), Turku, 1931–32. First
architectural chair design using moulded plywood
panel. Armchair 31 (cat.15), Turku, 1931–32.
Shelf-Table 111 (cat.16), Turku, 1935–36.

GERALD SUMMERS

Designer, furniture maker and manufacturer.
Born 1899, England. Died 1967, England.
Founded Makers of Simple Furniture Ltd,
Charlotte Street, London, in 1929.
Furniture designer in the 1930s. Produced, among
others, plywood chair with upholstered seat in
1935.
Author of an article on plywood furniture in *Design
for Today*, June 1935.
Abandoned furniture for the manufacture of
ballbearings by the Second World War.
Furniture designs include:
Armchair (cat.17), England, 1933/34.
Tea trolley, England, c.1935.

JEAN PROUVÉ

Constructor, designer.
Born 1901, Paris. Died 1984, Nancy.
Trained as metal worker in workshop of Emile
Robert.
Pupil of Szabo in Paris.
Installed his first studio in rue Général Custine,
Nancy.
*Diplome d'honneur, Exposition Internationale des
Arts Décoratifs*, Paris, 1925.
First encounter with Le Corbusier, Mallet-Stevens
and Pierre Jeanneret in 1926.
Workshop in rue des Jardiniers in Nancy – Les
Ateliers Jean Prouvé, 1931–44.
Established the Atelier de Maxéville, 1947–1953.
From 1949 Steph Simon became commercial
agent and representative for distribution of Prouvé
furniture.
In 1954 moved to Paris as consultant on major
building projects.
Installation of Galerie Steph Simon representing
Prouvé and Perriand furniture, 1956.
President of the Jury of the *Concours International
du Centre Pompidou*, 1971.
**Buildings on which Prouvé collaborated or which
he designed include:**
Collaboration on Maison du Peuple, Clichy, Paris,
1937–39.
Demountable housing for French Army, 1938.
Industrialised aluminium houses at Meudon, 1949
Communist Party Headquarters, Paris, with Oscar
Niemeyer, 1970.
Interiors and furniture design include:
Furniture for University of Nancy, 1932–33.
'Fauteuil Visiteur' Armchair (cat.22), Nancy, 1942
Chair 300 (cat.23), Nancy, c.1948.
'Antony' Chair (cat.24), Nancy, 1950.
Table 'Caféteria' (cat.25), Nancy, 1951
'Mexico' Double-fronted bookcase (cat.26),
Nancy, 1952.

SVEN MARKELIUS
Architect, town planner.
Born 1889, Stockholm. Died 1972, Stockholm.
Studied at the Stockholm Technical College and at the Royal Academy of Fine Arts, Stockholm.
City architect and planner to Stockholm, 1944–54.
Buildings include:
Villa Engkvist, Stockholm, 1929.
Exhibition buildings at Stockholm Fair, 1930.
Concert hall, at Helsingborg, 1932.
Swedish Pavilion at New York World's Fair, 1939.
Vällingby suburb with innovative pedestrian zone, 1953–59.
Interiors and furniture design include:
Stapelbara stol, Stockholm, c.1930.
Writing Desk and Chair (cat.13) and Chair, Stockholm, 1930.
EPA Bar, Stockholm, 1936.

CHARLES EAMES
Furniture and exhibition designer, film maker, architect.
Born 1907, St. Louis, Missouri.
Died 1978, St. Louis, Missouri.
Studied architecture at Washington University in St Louis.
Opened architectural office in 1930.
From 1936 taught at Cranbrook Academy of Art, Bloomfield Hills, Michigan; met Eero Saarinen.
In 1941 moved with his wife and collaborator, Ray Kaiser, to Southern California.
Commission by US Army to make plywood stretchers, splints, 1941–45.
Eames's buildings include:
Eames House and Studio, Pacific Palisades, Santa Monica, 1949.
House for neighbour, John Entenza, 1949.
Furniture designs include:
Together with Eero Saarinen, first prize for chair design at the Museum of Modern Art's Organic Furniture Competition, New York, 1940.
Folding Screen FSW6 (cat.27), California, 1946.
Second prize at the Museum of Modern Art's International Competition for Low-Cost Furniture.
Design for his one-piece 'Shell' Chair, made of fiberglass reinforced plastic, 1948.
Rocker RAR (cat.29), in moulded polyester, California, 1950.
'Surf Board' Table ETR (cat.28), California, 1952.
Lounge chair and ottoman, California, 1956.

VERNER PANTON
Architect, designer.
Born 1926 in Denmark. Lives in Switzerland.
Studied at Technical School, Odense, and Royal Danish Academy of Fine Arts, Copenhagen.
Worked as associate with Arne Jacobsen, 1950–52.
In 1955, started own design office in Switzerland.
Interiors and furniture design include:
Stacking Chairs (cat.30), formed from single sheet of polyester, Denmark, 1960.
Exhibition designs *Visiona 1* and *Visiona 2* for Bayer Chemicals, Cologne.
Spherical television set for Brionvega, 1963.

OLIVIER MOURGUE
Furniture, textile, and industrial designer.
Born 1939.
Studied interior design at the Ecole Boulle and at the Ecole Nationale Supérieure des Arts Décoratifs, Paris.
Since 1959 freelance designer.
In 1976 moved from Paris to Brittany, teaching at Ecole d'Art in Brest.
Eurodomus and AID awards, 1968.
Interiors and furniture designs include:
Djinn Series (cat.32), first furniture to move toward sculptural and flowing forms, using urethane foam over tubular steel frames, Paris, 1965.
Interior of French Pavilion, Montreal Expo, 1967.
'Bouloum' Lounge Chair, France, 1968.
Interior of French Pavilion, Osaka Expo, 1970.

PIERRE PAULIN
Furniture designer.
Born 1927.
In the 1950s designed for Thonet.
Since mid Sixties heads own industrial and interior design firm.
In 1968 collaboration with Mobilier National on study of new furniture.
Interiors and furniture design include:
Ribbon Chair, France, 1966.
Easy Chair 577 (cat.33), sculptural furniture with inner structure of steel tubing, covered in foam and upholstered in stretch fabric, France, 1966.
'Endless' Sofa, 1971.
Special Seating for French Government pavilion at Osaka Expo, 1970.
Furniture for the Elysée Palace in Paris.
Visitor seating for the Louvre.

JOE COLOMBO
Industrial and furniture designer.
Born 1930, Milan. Died 1971, Milan.
Studied painting in Milan at the Accademia di Belle Arti di Brera and architecture at the Politecnico.
Worked as painter and sculptor.
Turned to industrial design, opened office in Milan, 1962.
Three medals at Milan Triennale, 1964.
Compasso d'Oro awards in 1967 and 1970.
AID International Design Award, 1968.
Furniture designs include:
Armchair 4801/5 (cat.31), Milan, 1965.
Additional System combinable lounge chair and ottoman (cat.34), Milan, 1968.

ILLUSTRATION SOURCES

1. *Gebogenes Holz: Konstruktive Entwürfe Wien 1840–1910*, Asenbaum/Hummel, Vienna, 1979, p.19
2. *Das Interieur*, vol.IV, 1903, p.77
3. *Fünfundzwanzig Jahre Postsparkasse*, Verlag der K.K. Postsparkasse, Vienna, 1908
4 above. Archives, Centraal Museum, Utrecht
4 below. Theodore M. Brown, *The Work of G. Rietveld, Architect*, A.W. Bruna & Zoon, Utrecht, 1958, p.94 (ill.106)
5 above. Thonet catalogue, 1929/30
5 below. *Bent Wood and Metal Furniture 1850–1946*, American Federation of Art, New York, 1987, p.153 (fig.5–54)
6 above. Thonet catalogue, 1935
6 below. Thonet catalogue, 1932
7. Thonet catalogue, 1935
8 above. P. Drijver and J. Niemeijer, *Rietveld Meubels om zelf te maken/werboek, How to construct Rietveld Furniture/Workbook*, 1986, p.37
8 below. Brown, *Rietveld, Architect*, as above, p.175, (cat.59)
9 above. Private collection
9 below. Thonet catalogue, 1930/31
10 above. Thonet catalogue, 1930/31
10 below. Private collection
11. Christopher Wilk, *Thonet: 150 Years of Furniture*, Barron's, New York, 1980, p.109, (ill.141)
12 above. Embru-Werke catalogue, Rüti, Zurich, 1936 (model 2072)
12 below. Friederike Mehlau-Wiebking, Arthur Rüegg, Ruggero Tropeano, *Schweizer Typenmöbel 1925–1935: Sigfried Giedion und die Wohnbedarf AG*, Institute for the History and Theory of Architecture, Zurich, gta Verlag, Zurich, 1989, p.45 (ill.8)
13 above. Eva Rudberg, *Sven Markelius, arkitekt*, Arkitektur Förlag, Stockholm, 1989, p.63
13 below. Private collection, Stockholm
14 above. *Alvar Aalto Furniture*, Museum of Finnish Architecture, Finnish Society of Crafts and Design, Artek, Helsinki, 1984, p.88, (ill.145)
14 below. *Bent Wood and Metal Furniture: 1850–1946*, as above, p.312, (fig.101A)
15 above. *Alvar Aalto Furniture*, as above, p.87 (ill.144)
15 below. *Bent Wood and Metal Furniture: 1850–1946*, as above, p.160 (fig.5–68)
16. *Decorative Art 1937: Yearbook of 'The Studio'*, G.G. Holme, London, 1937
17. *Architectural Review*, London, December 1935, p.194
18 above. Brown, *Rietveld, Architect*, as above, p.104 (ill.122)
18 below. Brown, *Rietveld, Architect*, as above, p.125 (ill.161)

19 above. *Das federnde Aluminium-Möbel*, catalogue, Wohnbedarf, Zurich, 1933, cover
19 below. Mehlau-Wiebking, Rüegg, Tropeano, *Schweizer Typenmöbel 1925–1935*, as above, p.49, (ill.3)
20 above. *Bent Wood and Metal Furniture: 1850–1946*, p.159, (fig.5–67)
20 below. Christopher Wilk, *Marcel Breuer: Furniture and Interiors*, Museum of Modern Art, New York, 1981, p.145 (fig.147)
21. Wilk, *Marcel Breuer*, as above, p.149 (fig.153)
22 above. *Jean Prouvé, Serge Mouille: Two Master Metal Workers*, New York/Paris, 1985, p.56
22 below. *Jean Prouvé, Meubles 1924–1953*, Musée des Arts Décoratifs de Bordeaux, 1989, p.40
23. Jean Prouvé archive, University of Stuttgart, Prof. Dipl. Ing. Architekt Peter Sulzer
24. Jean Prouvé archive, University of Stuttgart
25 above. Jean Prouvé archive, University of Stuttgart
25 below. *L'Architecture d'Aujourd'hui*, 37, October 1951, p.xlvi
26. *Jean Prouvé 'Constructeur'*, Centre Georges Pompidou, Paris, 1990, p.187, (ADMM, photo J.C. Planchet/CC1)
27 above. Arthur Drexler, *Charles Eames: Furniture from the Design Collection*, Museum of Modern Art, New York, 1973, p.28, ill.46
27 below. Drexler, *Charles Eames*, as above, p.20, (ill.32)
28 above. Herman Miller catalogue, 1952
28 below. Herman Miller catalogue, 1952
29. Herman Miller catalogue, 1952
30 above. Gerd Hatje and Elke Kaspar, eds., *new furniture/neue möbel 9*, Verlag Gerd Hatje, Stuttgart, 1969, ill.19
30 below. Karl Mang, *Geschichte des modernen Möbels*, Verlag Gerd Hatje, Stuttgart, 1978, p.159, (ill.363)
31. *Italy: The New Domestic Landscape*, Museum of Modern Art, New York, 1972, p.30
32. Ted Sennett: *Great Hollywood Movies*, Abrams, New York, 1983, p.166
33 left. Gerd Hatje and Elke Kaspar, eds., *new furniture/neue möbel 8*, Verlag Gerd Hatje, Stuttgart, 1966, back pages
33 right. Gerd Hatje and Elke Kaspar, eds., *new furniture/neue möbel 9*, Verlag Gerd Hatje, Stuttgart, 1969, p.18, (ills.33–35)
34 above. *Italy: The New Domestic Landscape*, Museum of Modern Art, New York, 1972, p.116
34 below. Karl Mang, *Geschichte des modernen Möbels*, Verlag Gerd Hatje, Stuttgart, 1978, p.163 (ill.367)

Note:
The photographs of designers have been taken largely from *Modern Chairs 1918–1970*, Lund Humphries / Whitechapel Art Gallery, London 1970.

We are grateful to those individuals and institutions who have allowed us to reproduce illustrations. We regret that in some cases it has not been possible to trace the original copyright holders of photographs in earlier publications.